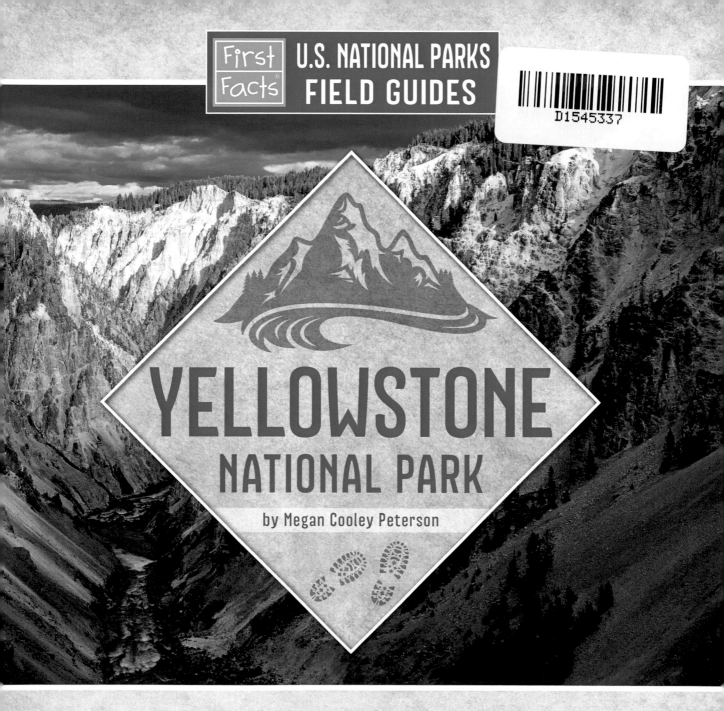

D1545337

YELLOWSTONE
NATIONAL PARK

by Megan Cooley Peterson

PEBBLE
a capstone imprint

First Facts Books are published by Pebble,
1710 Roe Crest Drive, North Mankato, Minnesota 56003
www.mycapstone.com

Library of Congress Cataloging-in-Publication Data is available
on the Library of Congress website.
ISBN 978-1-9771-0358-1 (library binding)
ISBN 978-1-9771-0528-8 (paperback)
ISBN 978-1-9771-0365-9 (ebook pdf)

Editorial Credits:
Anna Butzer, editor
Juliette Peters, designer
Tracy Cummins, media researcher
Kathy McColley, production specialist

Photo Credits:
Capstone: Eric Gohl, 9 Bottom, 11, 15, 17 Bottom, 21 Bottom;
National Park Service: 13 Bottom; Shutterstock: Benny Marty, 12,
Bertl123, 16–17, Berzina, 5 Top, BGSmith, 22–23, 24, Cat_arch_
angel, Design Element, chris kolaczan, 18 Left, Christine Krahl,
Design Element, DM Larson, 3 Bottom, 8 Top, Dmitry Kovba, 10–11,
EastVillage Images, Cover Bottom Right, Filip Fuxa, 6–7, Jake Eveler,
1, janaph, 5 Bottom, Jason Kolenda, 18–19, Jeff Holcombe, Cover
Bottom Middle, jo Crebbin, 13 Top, Kate_N, 9 Top, KGrif, 19 Top,
Kris Wiktor, 20–21, Lorcel, 3 Top, 3 Middle, Lucky-photographer,
2–3, NottomanV1, Design Element, Orhan Cam, Back Cover, Cover
Top, Pam Miller, 21 Top, Poul Riishede, 14–15, Roman Khomlyak,
7, 17 Top, Susanne Pommer, Cover Bottom Left, Tyler Hulett, 8
Bottom, viewgene, Design Element, Vlad Klok, Design Element

Printed and bound in the USA.
1335

Table of Contents

Welcome to Yellowstone

Yellowstone National Park sits on top of the largest active **volcano** on Earth. **Magma** heats up water under the ground. The boiling water pushes upward. Steam rises out of the cracks in the earth. Puddles of mud boil. **Geysers** shoot water into the air. There's never a dull moment at Yellowstone!

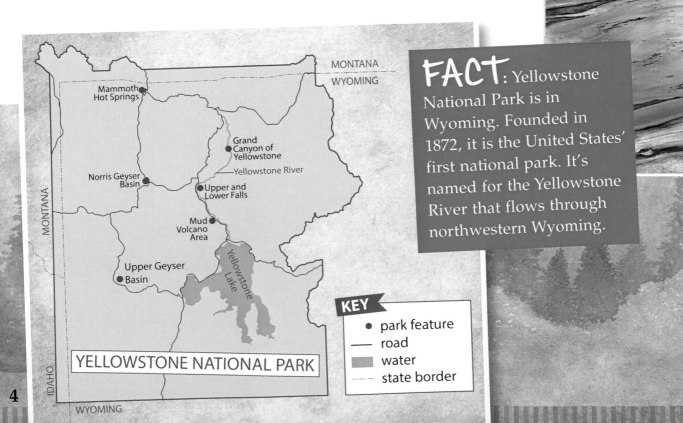

MONTANA
WYOMING

Mammoth Hot Springs

Grand Canyon of Yellowstone

Yellowstone River

Norris Geyser Basin

Upper and Lower Falls

MONTANA

Mud Volcano Area

Upper Geyser Basin

Yellowstone Lake

YELLOWSTONE NATIONAL PARK

IDAHO

WYOMING

KEY
- • park feature
- — road
- ▬ water
- ‑‑‑ state border

FACT: Yellowstone National Park is in Wyoming. Founded in 1872, it is the United States' first national park. It's named for the Yellowstone River that flows through northwestern Wyoming.

The Grand Prismatic Spring is the largest hot spring in the United States.

^ Castle Geyser

volcano—an opening in Earth's surface that sometimes sends out hot lava, steam, and ash

magma—melted rock found beneath the surface of Earth

geyser—a hot, underground spring from which steam and hot water shoot into the air

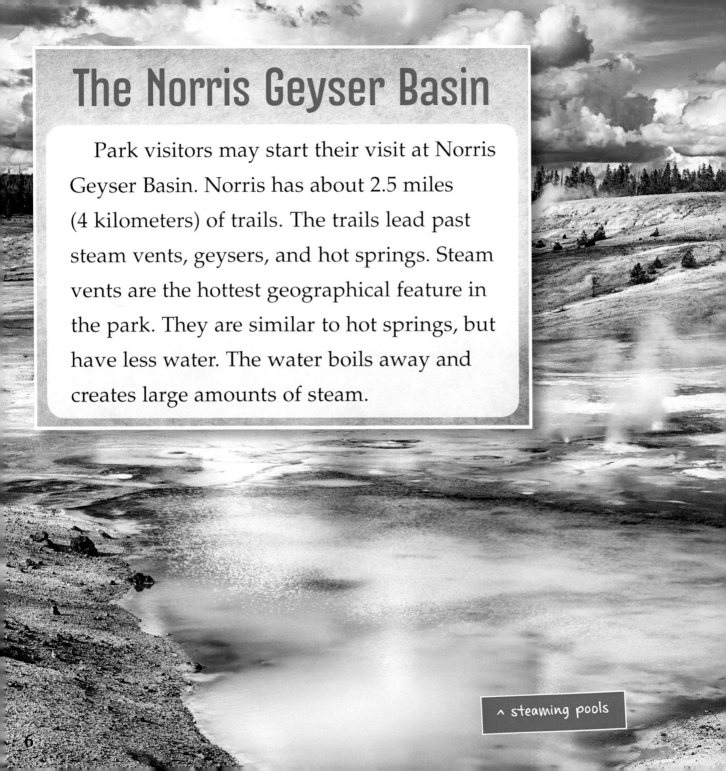

The Norris Geyser Basin

Park visitors may start their visit at Norris Geyser Basin. Norris has about 2.5 miles (4 kilometers) of trails. The trails lead past steam vents, geysers, and hot springs. Steam vents are the hottest geographical feature in the park. They are similar to hot springs, but have less water. The water boils away and creates large amounts of steam.

^ steaming pools

FACT: There are more than 15 miles (24 km) of **boardwalk** in Yellowstone National Park. These wooden planks allow visitors to safely see the different features of the park.

boardwalk—a raised wooden walkway

Emerald Spring sits in the Norris Geyser Back Basin. Steam rises from bubbling green-blue waters. Yellow **sulfur** lines the 27-foot (8-meter) deep pool.

sulfur—odorless and tasteless chemical element that has a pale yellowish color

FACT: While hiking, visitors may spot sagebrush lizards. The sagebrush is the only lizard that lives at Yellowstone.

Visitors can follow the Back Basin Trail about 600 feet (183 m) south to Steamboat Geyser. It is Yellowstone's tallest active geyser. It shoots water more than 300 feet (91 m) into the air. But it doesn't **erupt** often.

∧ Steamboat Geyser

erupt—to suddenly burst

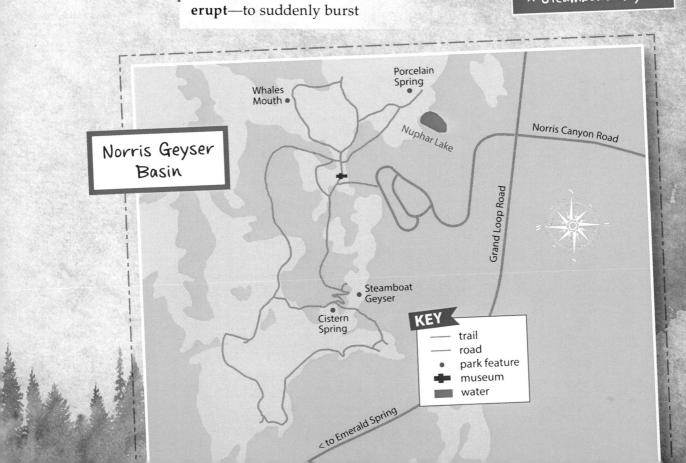

Norris Geyser Basin

Porcelain Spring

Whales Mouth •

Nuphar Lake

Norris Canyon Road

Grand Loop Road

Steamboat Geyser

Cistern Spring

KEY

— trail
— road
• park feature
✚ museum
▬ water

< to Emerald Spring

The Upper Geyser Basin

More than 250 geysers are found in the Upper Geyser Basin. It is home to Old Faithful, Yellowstone's most famous feature.

FACT: Yellowstone has more than 500 active geysers. The park has the largest number of geysers in the world.

Old Faithful ^

Many people stop at the Old Faithful visitor center to wait for the geyser to erupt. First, puffs of steam come up from the ground. Then water shoots 200 feet (61 m) into the air! Old Faithful erupts every 60 to 90 minutes.

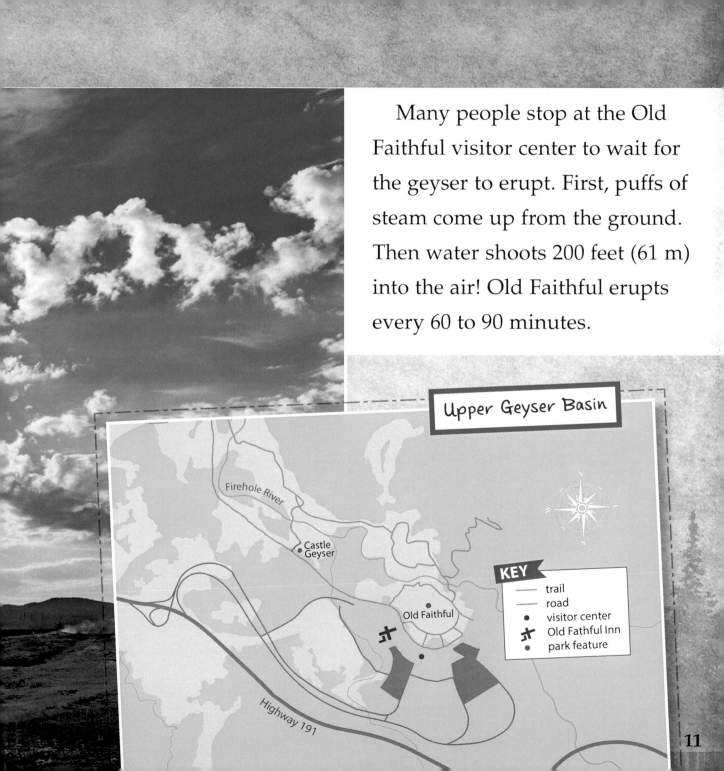

Upper Geyser Basin

Firehole River

Castle Geyser

Old Faithful

KEY
— trail
— road
• visitor center
✈ Old Fathful Inn
• park feature

Highway 191

∧ Castle Geyser

The Upper Geyser Basin has about 3 miles (4.8 km) of trails. Visitors can start at the Old Faithful Inn and hike the paved trail north to Castle Geyser. This geyser erupts about every 14 hours.

^ bison near the Firehole River

Visitors to Castle Geyser can follow the boardwalk over the Firehole River. Warm water from the geysers flow into the river, so it never freezes. In the winter, elk and bison drink from it.

FACT: The rare Yellowstone sulfur flower can be found near the Firehole River. This flower lives on land that is warm. It has only ever been seen in Yellowstone National Park.

Mammoth Hot Springs

Many visitors start their hike to Mammoth Hot Springs at Liberty Cap. Liberty Cap's 37-foot (11-m) tall rock is a hot spring that is no longer active. Visitors will hike uphill past **terraces** and hot springs. The hot springs leave behind liquid **limestone**. The limestone cools and hardens into terraces.

FACT: The Mammoth Hot Springs smell like rotten eggs. The smell comes from sulfur mixing with water in the hot springs.

Mammoth Hot Springs

KEY
- • park feature
- — trail
- — road
- — river
- ▨ Mammoth Area

Liberty Cap •

Grand Loop Road

Upper Terace Loop Drive

Canary Spring

N E W S

< terraces

terrace—a raised, flat platform of land with sloping sides

limestone—a hard rock formed from the remains of ancient sea creatures

15

Grand Canyon of the Yellowstone

The Grand Canyon of the Yellowstone is located in the south-east corner of the park. The canyon starts at the Lower Falls of the Yellowstone River. The Lower Falls drop 308 feet (94 m). The Yellowstone River flows through the canyon.

⌃ Lower Falls

To see the Lower Falls, visitors can hike up Uncle Tom's Trail. A set of 300 metal stairs lead the way to the bottom of the falls.

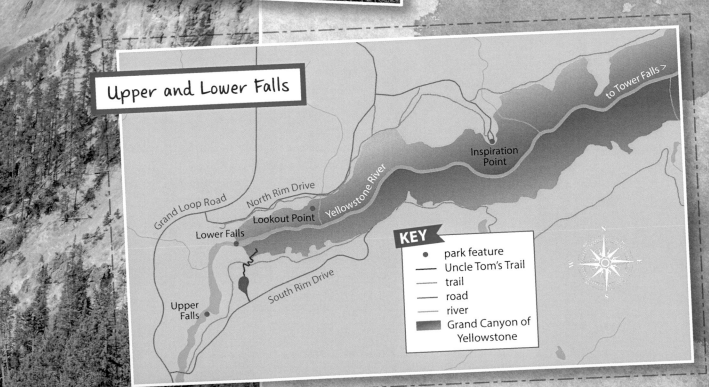

Upper and Lower Falls

Grand Loop Road

North Rim Drive

Lookout Point

Yellowstone River

Inspiration Point

to Tower Falls >

Lower Falls

South Rim Drive

Upper Falls

KEY
- park feature
- Uncle Tom's Trail
- trail
- road
- river
- Grand Canyon of Yellowstone

^ Tower Falls

The canyon ends at Tower Falls. Visitors can stand at the Tower Falls Overlook and watch the falls drop 132 feet (40 m). The trail down to the falls has been washed away. It's no longer safe to use.

^ osprey

The canyon has many other viewing areas. From Lookout Point, visitors can see birds flying. One of the most common is the osprey. Visitors might see osprey swoop down to grab fish from the Yellowstone River.

FACT: The Grand Canyon of Yellowstone National Park is about 20 miles (32 km) long.

Mud Volcano Area

Is there a dragon hiding in Yellowstone? No, it's the Dragon's Mouth Spring! From Grand Loop Road, visitors can hike the boardwalk to the spring. Steam hisses from a cave that looks like a dragon's mouth.

FACT: Only 24 bison lived in Yellowstone National Park in 1902. People hunted them illegally. The U.S. Army began protecting the bison shortly after. Today thousands of bison live in the park.

Continue north on the boardwalk and visit Mud Volcano. **Acid** in the groundwater has turned the rocks into mud. The gasses bubbling up through the **sludge** look like boiling soup. These are just a few of the amazing sights found only in Yellowstone National Park.

∧ Mud Volcano

acid—a strong liquid that can damage things it comes in contact with
sludge—wet, muddy mixture

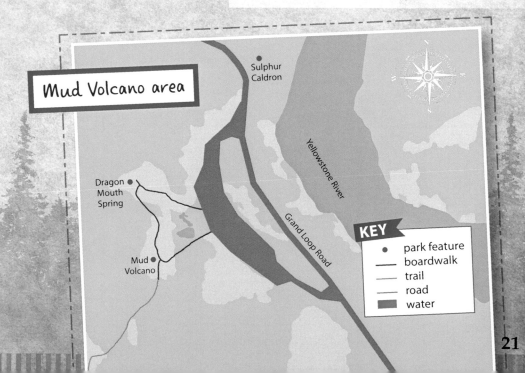

Mud Volcano area

Sulphur Caldron

Yellowstone River

Dragon Mouth Spring

Grand Loop Road

Mud Volcano

KEY
- • park feature
- — boardwalk
- trail
- road
- water

Glossary

acid (A-suhd)—a strong liquid that can damage things it comes in contact with

boardwalk (BORD-wawk)—raised wooden walkways

erupt (i-RUHPT)—to suddenly burst

geyser (GYE-zur)—a hot, underground spring from which steam and hot water shoot into the air

limestone (LIME-stohn)—a hard rock formed from the remains of ancient sea creatures

magma (MAG-muh)—melted rock found beneath the surface of Earth

sludge (SLUDJ)—wet, muddy mixture

sulfur (SUHL-fur)—odorless and tasteless chemical element that has a pale yellowish color

terrace (TER-iss)—a raised, flat platform of land with sloping sides

volcano (vol-KAY-noh)—an opening in Earth's surface that sometimes sends out hot lava, steam, and ash

Read More

McCarthy, Cecilia Pinto. *Yellowstone National Park.* National Parks. Minneapolis: Abdo Publishing, 2017.

Nagle, Frances. *Yellowstone National Park.* Road Trip: National Parks. New York: Gareth Stevens Publishing, 2016.

Wallace, Audra. *Yellowstone National Park.* National Parks. New York: Children's Press, 2018.

Internet Sites

Use FactHound to find Internet sites related to this book:

Visit *www.facthound.com*

Just type in 9781977103581 and go.

Check out projects, games and lots more at
www.capstonekids.com

Critical Thinking Questions

1. Describe a geyser. Use the photos and text to help you.

2. Which feature in Yellowstone National Park would you most like to see? Why?

3. Yellowstone is home to different plants, animals, and geographical features. What are some things you can find here that are unique to this park?

Index